Coffee Tasting Journal

DETAILS

NAME

ADDRESS

E-MAIL ADDRESS

WEBSITE

PHONE   **FAX**

EMERGENCY CONTACT PERSON

PHONE   **FAX**

Coffee Tasting Journal

Date ....

Coffee Name ....

Brand ....

Country / Region of Origin ....

Cost .... Purchased from ....

BREW METHOD	BREW TIME	AROMA / TASTE

Would I buy again?   ☐ Yes   ☐ No

NOTES

....
....
....
....
....
....
....
....

Rating ⭐ ⭐ ⭐ ⭐ ⭐

Coffee Tasting Journal

Date ....

Coffee Name ....

Brand ....

Country / Region of Origin ....

Cost .... Purchased from ....

BREW METHOD	BREW TIME	AROMA / TASTE

Would I buy again?   ☐ Yes   ☐ No

NOTES

....
....
....
....
....
....
....
....

Rating ⭐ ⭐ ⭐ ⭐ ⭐

Coffee Tasting Journal

Date ....

Coffee Name ....

Brand ....

Country / Region of Origin ....

Cost .... Purchased from ....

BREW METHOD	BREW TIME	AROMA / TASTE

Would I buy again? ☐ Yes   ☐ No

NOTES

....
....
....
....
....
....
....
....

Rating ★ ★ ★ ★ ★

Coffee Tasting Journal

Date ....

Coffee Name ....

Brand ....

Country / Region of Origin ....

Cost .... Purchased from ....

BREW METHOD	BREW TIME	AROMA / TASTE

Would I buy again?   ☐ Yes   ☐ No

NOTES

....
....
....
....
....
....
....
....
....

Rating ☆ ☆ ☆ ☆ ☆

Coffee Tasting Journal

Date ....

Coffee Name ....

Brand ....

Country / Region of Origin ....

Cost .... Purchased from ....

BREW METHOD	BREW TIME	AROMA / TASTE

Would I buy again? ☐ Yes   ☐ No

NOTES

....
....
....
....
....
....
....

Rating

Coffee Tasting Journal

Date ....

Coffee Name ....

Brand ....

Country / Region of Origin ....

Cost .... Purchased from ....

BREW METHOD	BREW TIME	AROMA / TASTE

Would I buy again?   ☐ Yes   ☐ No

NOTES

....
....
....
....
....
....
....
....

Rating ☆ ☆ ☆ ☆ ☆

Coffee Tasting Journal

Date ....

Coffee Name ....

Brand ....

Country / Region of Origin ....

Cost .... Purchased from ....

BREW METHOD	BREW TIME	AROMA / TASTE

Would I buy again?   ☐ Yes   ☐ No

NOTES

....
....
....
....
....
....
....
....
....

 Rating

Coffee Tasting Journal

Date ....

Coffee Name ....

Brand ....

Country / Region of Origin ....

Cost .... Purchased from ....

BREW METHOD	BREW TIME	AROMA / TASTE

Would I buy again?   ☐ Yes   ☐ No

NOTES
....
....
....
....
....
....
....
....

Rating ☆ ☆ ☆ ☆ ☆

Coffee Tasting Journal

Date ....

Coffee Name ....

Brand ....

Country / Region of Origin ....

Cost .... Purchased from ....

BREW METHOD	BREW TIME	AROMA / TASTE

Would I buy again?   ☐ Yes   ☐ No

NOTES

....
....
....
....
....
....
....
....

Rating

Coffee Tasting Journal

Date ....

Coffee Name ....

Brand ....

Country / Region of Origin ....

Cost .... Purchased from ....

BREW METHOD	BREW TIME	AROMA / TASTE

Would I buy again?   ☐ Yes   ☐ No

NOTES

....
....
....
....
....
....
....
....

Rating   ☆ ☆ ☆ ☆ ☆

Coffee Tasting Journal

Date ....

Coffee Name ....

Brand ....

Country / Region of Origin ....

Cost .... Purchased from ....

BREW METHOD	BREW TIME	AROMA / TASTE

Would I buy again?   ☐ Yes   ☐ No

NOTES

....
....
....
....
....
....
....
....

Rating

Coffee Tasting Journal

Date ....

Coffee Name ....

Brand ....

Country / Region of Origin ....

Cost .... Purchased from ....

BREW METHOD	BREW TIME	AROMA / TASTE

Would I buy again?   ☐ Yes   ☐ No

NOTES

....
....
....
....
....
....
....
....

Rating ☆ ☆ ☆ ☆ ☆

Coffee Tasting Journal

Date ....

Coffee Name ....

Brand ....

Country / Region of Origin ....

Cost .... Purchased from ....

BREW METHOD	BREW TIME	AROMA / TASTE

Would I buy again? ☐ Yes   ☐ No

NOTES

....
....
....
....
....
....
....
....
....

Rating ★ ★ ★ ★ ★

Coffee Tasting Journal

Date ....

Coffee Name ....

Brand ....

Country / Region of Origin ....

Cost .... Purchased from ....

BREW METHOD	BREW TIME	AROMA / TASTE

Would I buy again? ☐ Yes ☐ No

NOTES
....
....
....
....
....
....
....
....

Rating ☆ ☆ ☆ ☆ ☆

Coffee Tasting Journal

Date ....

Coffee Name ....

Brand ....

Country / Region of Origin ....

Cost .... Purchased from ....

BREW METHOD	BREW TIME	AROMA / TASTE

Would I buy again?   ☐ Yes   ☐ No

NOTES

....
....
....
....
....
....
....
....

Rating

Coffee Tasting Journal

Date ....

Coffee Name ....

Brand ....

Country / Region of Origin ....

Cost .... Purchased from ....

BREW METHOD	BREW TIME	AROMA / TASTE

Would I buy again? ☐ Yes   ☐ No

NOTES

....
....
....
....
....
....
....
....

Rating ☆ ☆ ☆ ☆ ☆

Coffee Tasting Journal

Date ....

Coffee Name ....

Brand ....

Country / Region of Origin ....

Cost .... Purchased from ....

BREW METHOD	BREW TIME	AROMA / TASTE

Would I buy again?   ☐ Yes   ☐ No

NOTES

....
....
....
....
....
....
....
....

Rating ★ ★ ★ ★ ★

Coffee Tasting Journal

Date ....

Coffee Name ....

Brand ....

Country / Region of Origin ....

Cost .... Purchased from ....

BREW METHOD	BREW TIME	AROMA / TASTE

Would I buy again?   ☐ Yes   ☐ No

NOTES

....
....
....
....
....
....
....
....

Rating ☆ ☆ ☆ ☆

Coffee Tasting Journal

Date ....

Coffee Name ....

Brand ....

Country / Region of Origin ....

Cost .... Purchased from ....

BREW METHOD	BREW TIME	AROMA / TASTE

Would I buy again?   ☐ Yes   ☐ No

NOTES

....
....
....
....
....
....
....
....

Rating ★ ★ ★ ★ ★

Coffee Tasting Journal

Date ....

Coffee Name ....

Brand ....

Country / Region of Origin ....

Cost .... Purchased from ....

BREW METHOD	BREW TIME	AROMA / TASTE

Would I buy again?   ☐ Yes   ☐ No

NOTES

....
....
....
....
....
....
....
....

Rating ⭐ ⭐ ⭐ ⭐ ⭐

Coffee Tasting Journal

Date ....

Coffee Name ....

Brand ....

Country / Region of Origin ....

Cost .... Purchased from ....

BREW METHOD	BREW TIME	AROMA / TASTE

Would I buy again?   ☐ Yes   ☐ No

NOTES

....
....
....
....
....
....
....
....

Rating ☆ ☆ ☆ ☆

Coffee Tasting Journal

Date ....

Coffee Name ....

Brand ....

Country / Region of Origin ....

Cost .... Purchased from ....

BREW METHOD	BREW TIME	AROMA / TASTE

Would I buy again? ☐ Yes   ☐ No

NOTES

....
....
....
....
....
....
....
....

Rating ☆ ☆ ☆ ☆ ☆

Coffee Tasting Journal

Date ....

Coffee Name ....

Brand ....

Country / Region of Origin ....

Cost .... Purchased from ....

BREW METHOD	BREW TIME	AROMA / TASTE

Would I buy again? ☐ Yes ☐ No

NOTES

....
....
....
....
....
....
....
....

Rating ★ ★ ★ ★ ★

Coffee Tasting Journal

Date ....

Coffee Name ....

Brand ....

Country / Region of Origin ....

Cost .... Purchased from ....

BREW METHOD	BREW TIME	AROMA / TASTE

Would I buy again? ☐ Yes   ☐ No

NOTES

Rating ★ ★ ★ ★ ★

Coffee Tasting Journal

Date ....

Coffee Name ....

Brand ....

Country / Region of Origin ....

Cost .... Purchased from ....

BREW METHOD	BREW TIME	AROMA / TASTE

Would I buy again?   ☐ Yes   ☐ No

NOTES

....
....
....
....
....
....
....
....

Rating

Coffee Tasting Journal

Date ....

Coffee Name ....

Brand ....

Country / Region of Origin ....

Cost .... Purchased from ....

BREW METHOD	BREW TIME	AROMA / TASTE

Would I buy again?   ☐ Yes   ☐ No

NOTES

....
....
....
....
....
....
....
....

Rating ⭐ ⭐ ⭐ ⭐ ⭐

Coffee Tasting Journal

Date ....

Coffee Name ....

Brand ....

Country / Region of Origin ....

Cost .... Purchased from ....

BREW METHOD	BREW TIME	AROMA / TASTE

Would I buy again?   ☐ Yes   ☐ No

NOTES

....
....
....
....
....
....
....
....

Rating ★ ★ ★ ★ ★

Coffee Tasting Journal

Date ....

Coffee Name ....

Brand ....

Country / Region of Origin ....

Cost .... Purchased from ....

BREW METHOD	BREW TIME	AROMA / TASTE

Would I buy again?   ☐ Yes   ☐ No

NOTES

....
....
....
....
....
....
....
....
....

Rating ☆ ☆ ☆ ☆ ☆

Coffee Tasting Journal

Date

Coffee Name ....

Brand ....

Country / Region of Origin ....

Cost .... Purchased from ....

BREW METHOD	BREW TIME	AROMA / TASTE

Would I buy again?   ☐ Yes   ☐ No

NOTES

....
....
....
....
....
....
....
....

Rating

Coffee Tasting Journal

Date ....

Coffee Name ....

Brand ....

Country / Region of Origin ....

Cost .... Purchased from ....

BREW METHOD	BREW TIME	AROMA / TASTE

Would I buy again?   ☐ Yes   ☐ No

NOTES

....
....
....
....
....
....
....
....

Rating   ★ ★ ★ ★ ★

Coffee Tasting Journal

Date ....

Coffee Name ....

Brand ....

Country / Region of Origin ....

Cost .... Purchased from ....

BREW METHOD	BREW TIME	AROMA / TASTE

Would I buy again?   ☐ Yes   ☐ No

NOTES

....
....
....
....
....
....
....
....

Rating ★ ★ ★ ★ ★

Coffee Tasting Journal

Date ....

Coffee Name ....

Brand ....

Country / Region of Origin ....

Cost .... Purchased from ....

BREW METHOD	BREW TIME	AROMA / TASTE

Would I buy again? ☐ Yes   ☐ No

NOTES

....
....
....
....
....
....
....
....

Rating ☆ ☆ ☆ ☆ ☆

Coffee Tasting Journal

Date

Coffee Name ....

Brand ....

Country / Region of Origin ....

Cost .... Purchased from ....

BREW METHOD	BREW TIME	AROMA / TASTE

Would I buy again? ☐ Yes   ☐ No

NOTES

....
....
....
....
....
....
....
....

 Rating

Coffee Tasting Journal

Date ....

Coffee Name ....

Brand ....

Country / Region of Origin ....

Cost .... Purchased from ....

BREW METHOD	BREW TIME	AROMA / TASTE

Would I buy again?   ☐ Yes   ☐ No

NOTES

....
....
....
....
....
....
....
....

Rating   ☆ ☆ ☆ ☆ ☆

Coffee Tasting Journal

Date ....

Coffee Name ....

Brand ....

Country / Region of Origin ....

Cost .... Purchased from ....

BREW METHOD	BREW TIME	AROMA / TASTE

Would I buy again?   ☐ Yes   ☐ No

NOTES

....
....
....
....
....
....
....

Rating ★ ★ ★ ★

Coffee Tasting Journal

Date ....

Coffee Name ....

Brand ....

Country / Region of Origin ....

Cost .... Purchased from ....

BREW METHOD	BREW TIME	AROMA / TASTE

Would I buy again?   ☐ Yes   ☐ No

NOTES

....
....
....
....
....
....
....
....

Rating ☆ ☆ ☆ ☆ ☆

Coffee Tasting Journal

Date ....

Coffee Name ....

Brand ....

Country / Region of Origin ....

Cost .... Purchased from ....

BREW METHOD	BREW TIME	AROMA / TASTE

Would I buy again?   ☐ Yes   ☐ No

NOTES

....
....
....
....
....
....
....
....

Rating

Coffee Tasting Journal

Date ....

Coffee Name ....

Brand ....

Country / Region of Origin ....

Cost .... Purchased from ....

BREW METHOD	BREW TIME	AROMA / TASTE

Would I buy again?   ☐ Yes   ☐ No

NOTES

....
....
....
....
....
....
....
....

Rating   ★ ★ ★ ★

Coffee Tasting Journal

Date ....

Coffee Name ....

Brand ....

Country / Region of Origin ....

Cost .... Purchased from ....

BREW METHOD	BREW TIME	AROMA / TASTE

Would I buy again?   ☐ Yes   ☐ No

NOTES

....
....
....
....
....
....
....
....

Rating ★ ★ ★ ★ ★

Coffee Tasting Journal

Date ....

Coffee Name ....

Brand ....

Country / Region of Origin ....

Cost .... Purchased from ....

BREW METHOD	BREW TIME	AROMA / TASTE

Would I buy again? ☐ Yes   ☐ No

NOTES

....
....
....
....
....
....
....
....

Rating ★ ★ ★ ★ ★

Coffee Tasting Journal

Date ....

Coffee Name ....

Brand ....

Country / Region of Origin ....

Cost .... Purchased from ....

BREW METHOD	BREW TIME	AROMA / TASTE

Would I buy again?   ☐ Yes   ☐ No

NOTES

....
....
....
....
....
....
....
....

 Rating

Coffee Tasting Journal

Date ....

Coffee Name ....

Brand ....

Country / Region of Origin ....

Cost .... Purchased from ....

BREW METHOD	BREW TIME	AROMA / TASTE

Would I buy again?   ☐ Yes   ☐ No

NOTES

....
....
....
....
....
....
....

Rating ☆ ☆ ☆ ☆ ☆

Coffee Tasting Journal

Date ....

Coffee Name ....

Brand ....

Country / Region of Origin ....

Cost .... Purchased from ....

BREW METHOD	BREW TIME	AROMA / TASTE

Would I buy again?   ☐ Yes   ☐ No

NOTES

....
....
....
....
....
....
....
....

Rating ★ ★ ★ ★ ★

Coffee Tasting Journal

Date ....

Coffee Name ....

Brand ....

Country / Region of Origin ....

Cost .... Purchased from ....

BREW METHOD	BREW TIME	AROMA / TASTE

Would I buy again?   ☐ Yes   ☐ No

NOTES

....
....
....
....
....
....
....
....

Rating ★ ★ ★ ★ ★

Coffee Tasting Journal

Date ....

Coffee Name ....

Brand ....

Country / Region of Origin ....

Cost .... Purchased from ....

BREW METHOD	BREW TIME	AROMA / TASTE

Would I buy again?   ☐ Yes   ☐ No

NOTES

....
....
....
....
....
....
....
....

Rating

Coffee Tasting Journal

Date ....

Coffee Name ....

Brand ....

Country / Region of Origin ....

Cost .... Purchased from ....

BREW METHOD	BREW TIME	AROMA / TASTE

Would I buy again?   ☐ Yes   ☐ No

NOTES

....
....
....
....
....
....
....
....

Rating   ☆ ☆ ☆ ☆ ☆

Coffee Tasting Journal

Date ....

Coffee Name ....

Brand ....

Country / Region of Origin ....

Cost .... Purchased from ....

BREW METHOD	BREW TIME	AROMA / TASTE

Would I buy again?   ☐ Yes   ☐ No

NOTES

....
....
....
....
....
....
....
....

Rating ★ ★ ★ ★ ★

Coffee Tasting Journal

Date ....

Coffee Name ....

Brand ....

Country / Region of Origin ....

Cost .... Purchased from ....

BREW METHOD	BREW TIME	AROMA / TASTE

Would I buy again?   ☐ Yes   ☐ No

NOTES

....
....
....
....
....
....
....
....
....

Rating ☆ ☆ ☆ ☆ ☆

Coffee Tasting Journal

Date ....

Coffee Name ....

Brand ....

Country / Region of Origin ....

Cost .... Purchased from ....

BREW METHOD	BREW TIME	AROMA / TASTE

Would I buy again?   ☐ Yes   ☐ No

NOTES

....
....
....
....
....
....
....
....

Rating

Coffee Tasting Journal

Date ....

Coffee Name ....

Brand ....

Country / Region of Origin ....

Cost .... Purchased from ....

BREW METHOD	BREW TIME	AROMA / TASTE

Would I buy again? ☐ Yes   ☐ No

NOTES

....
....
....
....
....
....
....
....

Rating ☆ ☆ ☆ ☆ ☆

Coffee Tasting Journal

Date ....

Coffee Name ....

Brand ....

Country / Region of Origin ....

Cost .... Purchased from ....

BREW METHOD	BREW TIME	AROMA / TASTE

Would I buy again?   ☐ Yes   ☐ No

NOTES

....
....
....
....
....
....
....
....

Rating ★ ★ ★ ★ ★

Coffee Tasting Journal

Date ....

Coffee Name ....

Brand ....

Country / Region of Origin ....

Cost .... Purchased from ....

BREW METHOD	BREW TIME	AROMA / TASTE

Would I buy again?   ☐ Yes   ☐ No

NOTES

....
....
....
....
....
....
....
....

Rating ★ ★ ★ ★ ★

Coffee Tasting Journal

Date

Coffee Name ....

Brand ....

Country / Region of Origin ....

Cost .... Purchased from ....

BREW METHOD	BREW TIME	AROMA / TASTE

Would I buy again?   ☐ Yes   ☐ No

NOTES

....
....
....
....
....
....
....
....

Rating

Coffee Tasting Journal

Date ....

Coffee Name ....

Brand ....

Country / Region of Origin ....

Cost .... Purchased from ....

BREW METHOD	BREW TIME	AROMA / TASTE

Would I buy again?   ☐ Yes   ☐ No

NOTES
....
....
....
....
....
....
....
....

Rating ☆ ☆ ☆ ☆ ☆

Coffee Tasting Journal

Date ....

Coffee Name ....

Brand ....

Country / Region of Origin ....

Cost .... Purchased from ....

BREW METHOD	BREW TIME	AROMA / TASTE

Would I buy again?   ☐ Yes   ☐ No

NOTES

....
....
....
....
....
....
....

Rating ★ ★ ★ ★ ★

Coffee Tasting Journal

Date ....

Coffee Name ....

Brand ....

Country / Region of Origin ....

Cost .... Purchased from ....

BREW METHOD	BREW TIME	AROMA / TASTE

Would I buy again?   ☐ Yes   ☐ No

NOTES

Rating ⭐ ⭐ ⭐ ⭐ ⭐

Coffee Tasting Journal

Date ....

Coffee Name ....

Brand ....

Country / Region of Origin ....

Cost .... Purchased from ....

BREW METHOD	BREW TIME	AROMA / TASTE

Would I buy again?   ☐ Yes   ☐ No

NOTES

....
....
....
....
....
....
....
....

Rating

Coffee Tasting Journal

Date ....

Coffee Name ....

Brand ....

Country / Region of Origin ....

Cost .... Purchased from ....

BREW METHOD	BREW TIME	AROMA / TASTE

Would I buy again?   ☐ Yes   ☐ No

NOTES

....
....
....
....
....
....
....
....

Rating ★ ★ ★ ★ ★

Coffee Tasting Journal

Date ....

Coffee Name ....

Brand ....

Country / Region of Origin ....

Cost .... Purchased from ....

BREW METHOD	BREW TIME	AROMA / TASTE

Would I buy again? ☐ Yes ☐ No

NOTES

....
....
....
....
....
....
....
....

Rating ★ ★ ★ ★ ★

Coffee Tasting Journal

Date ....

Coffee Name ....

Brand ....

Country / Region of Origin ....

Cost .... Purchased from ....

BREW METHOD	BREW TIME	AROMA / TASTE

Would I buy again?   ☐ Yes   ☐ No

NOTES

....
....
....
....
....
....
....
....

Rating

Coffee Tasting Journal

Date ....

Coffee Name ....

Brand ....

Country / Region of Origin ....

Cost .... Purchased from ....

BREW METHOD	BREW TIME	AROMA / TASTE

Would I buy again?   ☐ Yes   ☐ No

NOTES

....
....
....
....
....
....
....
....

Rating   ★ ★ ★ ★

Coffee Tasting Journal

Date ....

Coffee Name ....

Brand ....

Country / Region of Origin ....

Cost .... Purchased from ....

BREW METHOD	BREW TIME	AROMA / TASTE

Would I buy again?   ☐ Yes   ☐ No

NOTES

....
....
....
....
....
....
....
....

Rating ☆ ☆ ☆ ☆ ☆

Coffee Tasting Journal

Date ....

Coffee Name ....

Brand ....

Country / Region of Origin ....

Cost .... Purchased from ....

BREW METHOD	BREW TIME	AROMA / TASTE

Would I buy again? ☐ Yes ☐ No

NOTES

....
....
....
....
....
....
....
....

Rating ★ ★ ★ ★ ★

Coffee Tasting Journal  Date ....

Coffee Name ....

Brand ....

Country / Region of Origin ....

Cost .... Purchased from ....

BREW METHOD	BREW TIME	AROMA / TASTE

Would I buy again?   ☐ Yes   ☐ No

NOTES

....
....
....
....
....
....
....
....

Rating   ☆ ☆ ☆ ☆

Coffee Tasting Journal

Date

Coffee Name ....

Brand ....

Country / Region of Origin ....

Cost .... Purchased from ....

BREW METHOD	BREW TIME	AROMA / TASTE

Would I buy again?   ☐ Yes   ☐ No

NOTES

....
....
....
....
....
....
....
....

Rating

Coffee Tasting Journal

Date ....

Coffee Name ....

Brand ....

Country / Region of Origin ....

Cost .... Purchased from ....

BREW METHOD	BREW TIME	AROMA / TASTE

Would I buy again?   ☐ Yes   ☐ No

NOTES

....
....
....
....
....
....
....
....

Rating ★ ★ ★ ★ ★

Coffee Tasting Journal

Date ....

Coffee Name ....

Brand ....

Country / Region of Origin ....

Cost .... Purchased from ....

BREW METHOD	BREW TIME	AROMA / TASTE

Would I buy again?   ☐ Yes   ☐ No

NOTES

....
....
....
....
....
....
....
....

Rating ★ ★ ★ ★

Coffee Tasting Journal

Date ....

Coffee Name ....

Brand ....

Country / Region of Origin ....

Cost .... Purchased from ....

BREW METHOD	BREW TIME	AROMA / TASTE

Would I buy again?   ☐ Yes   ☐ No

NOTES
....
....
....
....
....
....
....
....
....

Rating   ☆ ☆ ☆ ☆ ☆

Coffee Tasting Journal

Date ....

Coffee Name ....

Brand ....

Country / Region of Origin ....

Cost .... Purchased from ....

BREW METHOD	BREW TIME	AROMA / TASTE

Would I buy again?   ☐ Yes   ☐ No

NOTES

....
....
....
....
....
....
....
....

 Rating

Coffee Tasting Journal

Date ....

Coffee Name ....

Brand ....

Country / Region of Origin ....

Cost .... Purchased from ....

BREW METHOD	BREW TIME	AROMA / TASTE

Would I buy again?   ☐ Yes   ☐ No

NOTES

....
....
....
....
....
....
....
....

Rating ★ ★ ★ ★ ★

Coffee Tasting Journal

Date ....

Coffee Name ....

Brand ....

Country / Region of Origin ....

Cost .... Purchased from ....

BREW METHOD	BREW TIME	AROMA / TASTE

Would I buy again?   ☐ Yes   ☐ No

NOTES

....
....
....
....
....
....
....
....

Rating ★ ★ ★ ★ ★

Coffee Tasting Journal

Date ....

Coffee Name ....

Brand ....

Country / Region of Origin ....

Cost .... Purchased from ....

BREW METHOD	BREW TIME	AROMA / TASTE

Would I buy again? ☐ Yes   ☐ No

NOTES

....
....
....
....
....
....
....
....
....

Rating ☆ ☆ ☆ ☆ ☆

Coffee Tasting Journal

Date ....

Coffee Name ....

Brand ....

Country / Region of Origin ....

Cost .... Purchased from ....

BREW METHOD	BREW TIME	AROMA / TASTE

Would I buy again? ☐ Yes   ☐ No

NOTES

....
....
....
....
....
....
....

Rating

Coffee Tasting Journal

Date ....

Coffee Name ....

Brand ....

Country / Region of Origin ....

Cost .... Purchased from ....

BREW METHOD	BREW TIME	AROMA / TASTE

Would I buy again?   ☐ Yes   ☐ No

NOTES

....
....
....
....
....
....
....
....

Rating ☆ ☆ ☆ ☆ ☆

Coffee Tasting Journal

Date ....

Coffee Name ....

Brand ....

Country / Region of Origin ....

Cost .... Purchased from ....

BREW METHOD	BREW TIME	AROMA / TASTE

Would I buy again? ☐ Yes   ☐ No

NOTES

....
....
....
....
....
....
....
....

Rating ★ ★ ★ ★ ★

Coffee Tasting Journal

Date ....

Coffee Name ....

Brand ....

Country / Region of Origin ....

Cost .... Purchased from ....

BREW METHOD	BREW TIME	AROMA / TASTE

Would I buy again?   ☐ Yes   ☐ No

NOTES

....
....
....
....
....
....
....
....
....

Rating ☆ ☆ ☆ ☆ ☆

Coffee Tasting Journal

Date ....

Coffee Name ....

Brand ....

Country / Region of Origin ....

Cost .... Purchased from ....

BREW METHOD	BREW TIME	AROMA / TASTE

Would I buy again? ☐ Yes   ☐ No

NOTES
....
....
....
....
....
....
....
....

Rating

Coffee Tasting Journal

Date ....

Coffee Name ....

Brand ....

Country / Region of Origin ....

Cost .... Purchased from ....

BREW METHOD	BREW TIME	AROMA / TASTE

Would I buy again? ☐ Yes ☐ No

NOTES

....
....
....
....
....
....
....

Rating ☆ ☆ ☆ ☆ ☆

Coffee Tasting Journal

Date ....

Coffee Name ....

Brand ....

Country / Region of Origin ....

Cost .... Purchased from ....

BREW METHOD	BREW TIME	AROMA / TASTE

Would I buy again?   ☐ Yes   ☐ No

NOTES

....
....
....
....
....
....
....
....

Rating ★ ★ ★ ★ ★

Coffee Tasting Journal

Date ....

Coffee Name ....

Brand ....

Country / Region of Origin ....

Cost .... Purchased from ....

BREW METHOD	BREW TIME	AROMA / TASTE

Would I buy again?   ☐ Yes   ☐ No

NOTES

....
....
....
....
....
....
....
....

Rating ☆ ☆ ☆ ☆ ☆

Coffee Tasting Journal

Date ....

Coffee Name ....

Brand ....

Country / Region of Origin ....

Cost .... Purchased from ....

BREW METHOD	BREW TIME	AROMA / TASTE

Would I buy again? ☐ Yes ☐ No

NOTES

....
....
....
....
....
....
....
....

Rating ★ ★ ★ ★ ★

Coffee Tasting Journal  Date ....

Coffee Name ....

Brand ....

Country / Region of Origin ....

Cost .... Purchased from ....

BREW METHOD	BREW TIME	AROMA / TASTE

Would I buy again?   ☐ Yes   ☐ No

NOTES

....
....
....
....
....
....
....
....

Rating ★ ★ ★ ★ ★

Coffee Tasting Journal

Date ....

Coffee Name ....

Brand ....

Country / Region of Origin ....

Cost .... Purchased from ....

BREW METHOD	BREW TIME	AROMA / TASTE

Would I buy again?   ☐ Yes   ☐ No

NOTES

....
....
....
....
....
....
....
....

Rating ★ ★ ★ ★ ★

Coffee Tasting Journal

Date ....

Coffee Name ....

Brand ....

Country / Region of Origin ....

Cost .... Purchased from ....

BREW METHOD	BREW TIME	AROMA / TASTE

Would I buy again?   ☐ Yes   ☐ No

NOTES

....
....
....
....
....
....
....
....
....

Rating   ☆ ☆ ☆ ☆ ☆

Coffee Tasting Journal

Date ....

Coffee Name ....

Brand ....

Country / Region of Origin ....

Cost .... Purchased from ....

BREW METHOD	BREW TIME	AROMA / TASTE

Would I buy again? ☐ Yes   ☐ No

NOTES

....
....
....
....
....
....
....
....

Rating ⭐ ⭐ ⭐ ⭐ ⭐

Coffee Tasting Journal

Date ....

Coffee Name ....

Brand ....

Country / Region of Origin ....

Cost .... Purchased from ....

BREW METHOD	BREW TIME	AROMA / TASTE

Would I buy again? ☐ Yes ☐ No

NOTES

....
....
....
....
....
....
....
....

Rating ☆ ☆ ☆ ☆

Coffee Tasting Journal

Date ....

Coffee Name ....

Brand ....

Country / Region of Origin ....

Cost .... Purchased from ....

BREW METHOD	BREW TIME	AROMA / TASTE

Would I buy again?   ☐ Yes   ☐ No

NOTES

....
....
....
....
....
....
....
....

Rating ⭐ ⭐ ⭐ ⭐

Coffee Tasting Journal

Date ....

Coffee Name ....

Brand ....

Country / Region of Origin ....

Cost .... Purchased from ....

BREW METHOD	BREW TIME	AROMA / TASTE

Would I buy again?   ☐ Yes   ☐ No

NOTES

....
....
....
....
....
....
....
....

Rating ☆ ☆ ☆ ☆ ☆

Coffee Tasting Journal

Date ....

Coffee Name ....

Brand ....

Country / Region of Origin ....

Cost .... Purchased from ....

BREW METHOD	BREW TIME	AROMA / TASTE

Would I buy again?   ☐ Yes   ☐ No

NOTES

....
....
....
....
....
....
....
....

Rating ⭐ ⭐ ⭐ ⭐ ⭐

Coffee Tasting Journal

Date ....

Coffee Name ....

Brand ....

Country / Region of Origin ....

Cost .... Purchased from ....

BREW METHOD	BREW TIME	AROMA / TASTE

Would I buy again? ☐ Yes ☐ No

NOTES

....
....
....
....
....
....
....
....

Rating ☆ ☆ ☆ ☆ ☆

Coffee Tasting Journal

Date ....

Coffee Name ....

Brand ....

Country / Region of Origin ....

Cost .... Purchased from ....

BREW METHOD	BREW TIME	AROMA / TASTE

Would I buy again?   ☐ Yes   ☐ No

NOTES

....
....
....
....
....
....
....
....

Rating ★ ★ ★ ★ ★

Coffee Tasting Journal

Date ....

Coffee Name ....

Brand ....

Country / Region of Origin ....

Cost .... Purchased from ....

BREW METHOD	BREW TIME	AROMA / TASTE

Would I buy again?   ☐ Yes   ☐ No

NOTES

....
....
....
....
....
....
....
....

Rating   ☆ ☆ ☆ ☆

Coffee Tasting Journal

Date ....

Coffee Name ....

Brand ....

Country / Region of Origin ....

Cost .... Purchased from ....

BREW METHOD	BREW TIME	AROMA / TASTE

Would I buy again? ☐ Yes   ☐ No

NOTES

....
....
....
....
....
....
....
....

Rating

Coffee Tasting Journal

Date ....

Coffee Name ....

Brand ....

Country / Region of Origin ....

Cost .... Purchased from ....

BREW METHOD	BREW TIME	AROMA / TASTE

Would I buy again?   ☐ Yes   ☐ No

NOTES

....
....
....
....
....
....
....
....

Rating ☆ ☆ ☆ ☆ ☆

Coffee Tasting Journal

Date ....

Coffee Name ....

Brand ....

Country / Region of Origin ....

Cost .... Purchased from ....

BREW METHOD	BREW TIME	AROMA / TASTE

Would I buy again?   ☐ Yes   ☐ No

NOTES

....
....
....
....
....
....
....

Rating ★ ★ ★ ★ ★

Coffee Tasting Journal

Date ....

Coffee Name ....

Brand ....

Country / Region of Origin ....

Cost .... Purchased from ....

BREW METHOD	BREW TIME	AROMA / TASTE

Would I buy again?   ☐ Yes   ☐ No

NOTES

....
....
....
....
....
....
....
....
....

Rating ☆ ☆ ☆ ☆ ☆

Coffee Tasting Journal

Date ....

Coffee Name ....

Brand ....

Country / Region of Origin ....

Cost .... Purchased from ....

BREW METHOD	BREW TIME	AROMA / TASTE

Would I buy again?   ☐ Yes   ☐ No

NOTES

....
....
....
....
....
....
....
....

Rating ★ ★ ★ ★ ★

Coffee Tasting Journal  Date ....

Coffee Name ....

Brand ....

Country / Region of Origin ....

Cost .... Purchased from ....

BREW METHOD	BREW TIME	AROMA / TASTE

Would I buy again?   ☐ Yes   ☐ No

NOTES

....
....
....
....
....
....
....
....

Rating ☆ ☆ ☆ ☆ ☆

Coffee Tasting Journal

Date ....

Coffee Name ....

Brand ....

Country / Region of Origin ....

Cost .... Purchased from ....

BREW METHOD	BREW TIME	AROMA / TASTE

Would I buy again?   ☐ Yes   ☐ No

NOTES

....
....
....
....
....
....
....
....

Rating ★ ★ ★ ★ ★

Coffee Tasting Journal

Date ....

Coffee Name ....

Brand ....

Country / Region of Origin ....

Cost .... Purchased from ....

BREW METHOD	BREW TIME	AROMA / TASTE

Would I buy again?   ☐ Yes   ☐ No

NOTES

....
....
....
....
....
....
....
....

Rating   ☆ ☆ ☆ ☆ ☆

Coffee Tasting Journal

Date ....

Coffee Name ....

Brand ....

Country / Region of Origin ....

Cost .... Purchased from ....

BREW METHOD	BREW TIME	AROMA / TASTE

Would I buy again? ☐ Yes ☐ No

NOTES

....
....
....
....
....
....
....
....

Rating

Coffee Tasting Journal

Date ....

Coffee Name ....

Brand ....

Country / Region of Origin ....

Cost .... Purchased from ....

BREW METHOD	BREW TIME	AROMA / TASTE

Would I buy again?   ☐ Yes   ☐ No

NOTES

....
....
....
....
....
....
....
....

Rating ☆ ☆ ☆ ☆ ☆

Coffee Tasting Journal

Date ....

Coffee Name ....

Brand ....

Country / Region of Origin ....

Cost .... Purchased from ....

BREW METHOD	BREW TIME	AROMA / TASTE

Would I buy again?   ☐ Yes   ☐ No

NOTES

....
....
....
....
....
....
....
....

Rating

Coffee Tasting Journal

Date ....

Coffee Name ....

Brand ....

Country / Region of Origin ....

Cost .... Purchased from ....

BREW METHOD	BREW TIME	AROMA / TASTE

Would I buy again?   ☐ Yes   ☐ No

NOTES

....
....
....
....
....
....
....
....

Rating ★ ★ ★ ★ ★

Coffee Tasting Journal

Date

Coffee Name ....

Brand ....

Country / Region of Origin ....

Cost .... Purchased from ....

BREW METHOD	BREW TIME	AROMA / TASTE

Would I buy again?   ☐ Yes   ☐ No

NOTES

....
....
....
....
....
....
....
....

Rating ★ ★ ★ ★

Coffee Tasting Journal

Date ....

Coffee Name ....

Brand ....

Country / Region of Origin ....

Cost .... Purchased from ....

BREW METHOD	BREW TIME	AROMA / TASTE

Would I buy again?   ☐ Yes   ☐ No

NOTES

....
....
....
....
....
....
....
....
....

Rating ☆ ☆ ☆ ☆ ☆

Coffee Tasting Journal

Date ....

Coffee Name ....

Brand ....

Country / Region of Origin ....

Cost .... Purchased from ....

BREW METHOD	BREW TIME	AROMA / TASTE

Would I buy again?   ☐ Yes   ☐ No

NOTES

....
....
....
....
....
....
....

Rating

Coffee Tasting Journal

Date ....

Coffee Name ....

Brand ....

Country / Region of Origin ....

Cost .... Purchased from ....

BREW METHOD	BREW TIME	AROMA / TASTE

Would I buy again?   ☐ Yes   ☐ No

NOTES

....
....
....
....
....
....
....
....

Rating ☆ ☆ ☆ ☆ ☆

Coffee Tasting Journal

Date ....

Coffee Name ....

Brand ....

Country / Region of Origin ....

Cost .... Purchased from ....

BREW METHOD	BREW TIME	AROMA / TASTE

Would I buy again? ☐ Yes ☐ No

NOTES

....
....
....
....
....
....
....
....

 Rating

Coffee Tasting Journal

Date ....

Coffee Name ....

Brand ....

Country / Region of Origin ....

Cost .... Purchased from ....

BREW METHOD	BREW TIME	AROMA / TASTE

Would I buy again? ☐ Yes   ☐ No

NOTES

....
....
....
....
....
....
....
....

Rating ☆ ☆ ☆ ☆

Coffee Tasting Journal

Date ....

Coffee Name ....

Brand ....

Country / Region of Origin ....

Cost .... Purchased from ....

BREW METHOD	BREW TIME	AROMA / TASTE

Would I buy again?   ☐ Yes   ☐ No

NOTES

....
....
....
....
....
....
....
....

Rating   ★ ★ ★ ★

Coffee Tasting Journal

Date .....

Coffee Name ....

Brand ....

Country / Region of Origin ....

Cost .... Purchased from ....

BREW METHOD	BREW TIME	AROMA / TASTE

Would I buy again?   ☐ Yes   ☐ No

NOTES

....
....
....
....
....
....
....
....

Rating ★ ★ ★ ★ ★

Coffee Tasting Journal

Date ....

Coffee Name ....

Brand ....

Country / Region of Origin ....

Cost .... Purchased from ....

BREW METHOD	BREW TIME	AROMA / TASTE

Would I buy again?   ☐ Yes   ☐ No

NOTES

....
....
....
....
....
....
....
....

Rating ★ ★ ★ ★ ★

Coffee Tasting Journal  Date ....

Coffee Name ....

Brand ....

Country / Region of Origin ....

Cost .... Purchased from ....

BREW METHOD	BREW TIME	AROMA / TASTE

Would I buy again? ☐ Yes   ☐ No

NOTES
....
....
....
....
....
....
....
....

Rating   ☆ ☆ ☆ ☆

Coffee Tasting Journal

Date ....

Coffee Name ....

Brand ....

Country / Region of Origin ....

Cost .... Purchased from ....

BREW METHOD	BREW TIME	AROMA / TASTE

Would I buy again?   ☐ Yes   ☐ No

NOTES

....
....
....
....
....
....
....
....

Rating

Coffee Tasting Journal

Date ....

Coffee Name ....

Brand ....

Country / Region of Origin ....

Cost .... Purchased from ....

BREW METHOD	BREW TIME	AROMA / TASTE

Would I buy again?   ☐ Yes   ☐ No

NOTES

....
....
....
....
....
....
....
....

Rating ★ ★ ★ ★

Coffee Tasting Journal

Date ....

Coffee Name ....

Brand ....

Country / Region of Origin ....

Cost .... Purchased from ....

BREW METHOD	BREW TIME	AROMA / TASTE

Would I buy again?   ☐ Yes   ☐ No

NOTES

....
....
....
....
....
....
....
....

Rating

Coffee Tasting Journal

Date ....

Coffee Name ....

Brand ....

Country / Region of Origin ....

Cost .... Purchased from ....

BREW METHOD	**BREW TIME**	**AROMA / TASTE**

Would I buy again? ☐ Yes ☐ No

NOTES

....
....
....
....
....
....
....
....

Rating ☆ ☆ ☆ ☆ ☆

Coffee Tasting Journal

Date ....

Coffee Name ....

Brand ....

Country / Region of Origin ....

Cost .... Purchased from ....

BREW METHOD	BREW TIME	AROMA / TASTE

Would I buy again?   ☐ Yes   ☐ No

NOTES

....
....
....
....
....
....
....
....

Rating ☆ ☆ ☆ ☆ ☆

www.ingramcontent.com/pod-product-compliance
Lightning Source LLC
Chambersburg PA
CBHW081352080526
44588CB00016B/2461